Mysterious Encounters

Fortune-Telling

by Katherine E. Krohn

KIDHAVEN PRESS
A part of Gale, Cengage Learning

GALE
CENGAGE Learning™

Detroit • New York • San Francisco • New Haven, Conn • Waterville, Maine • London

LIBRARY OF CONGRESS CATALOGING-IN-PUBLICATION DATA

Krohn, Katherine E.
  Fortune-telling / by Katherine Krohn.
    p. cm. — (Mysterious encounters)
  Includes bibliographical references and index.
  ISBN 978-0-7377-4085-1 (hardcover)
  1. Fortune-telling—Juvenile literature. I. Title.
  BF1874.K76 2009
  133.3—dc22
                                                                 2008027341

KidHaven Press
27500 Drake Rd.
Farmington Hills, MI 48331

ISBN-13: 978-0-7377-4085-1
ISBN-10: 0-7377-4085-X

Printed in the United States of America
1 2 3 4 5 6 7 12 11 10 09 08

Contents

Chapter 1

Predicting the Future

People all over the world believe in fortune-telling. Fortune-telling is the ability to see into the future and predict coming events. People hire professional fortune-tellers because they want to know what is going to happen in their love lives, at their jobs, or with their health. Some people hire fortune-tellers just for fun or entertainment.

There are hundreds of ways to tell a fortune. **Astrology**, tarot cards, gazing into a crystal ball, and palm reading are common ways to foretell the future. Fortune-telling can also be done to find information about a person's personality or character. **Character reading** can be done by reading a person's face or handwriting.

Some individuals seek the advice of expensive telephone **psychics**, who charge callers' telephone accounts by the minute for psychic readings. Other people prefer to foretell their own fortune in simple, inexpensive ways. Many people read their daily horoscope in the newspaper. Popular toys such as

Fortune-tellers may use several different ways to look into the future, including the use of tarot cards.

Fishing for Fortunes

"Baiting" or "fishing" is a technique that dishonest fortune-tellers sometimes use. The fortune-teller first makes a general statement that could apply to many people. Then he or she watches for a response, fishing for information. The fortune-teller then makes up predictions based on the client's reaction. Baiters often make general statements that could apply to a wide variety of people, such as, "An elderly relative is expecting a letter from you," or, "You are hiding a secret."

the Magic 8 Ball or the Ouija board game are commonly used to tell fortunes. Chinese fortune cookies, which come along with their own small paper fortune, are enjoyed by many people.

Is It Real?

While some people believe in the ability to foretell the future, others do not. Skeptics of fortune-telling do not believe it is possible to know what is going to happen in the future. Scientists have not been able to prove in a laboratory setting that psychic ability exists.

Many scientific researchers have tried to prove that psychic ability is real. In the 1930s J.B. Rhine, a psychology professor at Duke University in North Carolina, and his wife, Louisa Rhine, conducted studies of **extrasensory perception (ESP)**. The term *ESP* referred to communication, or knowing something, by means other than our five physical senses. The Rhines called their area of study **parapsychology**.

The Rhines used a deck of cards to test the ESP abilities of volunteers. Each card had a picture of either a plus sign, a star, a square, wavy lines, or a circle. In the laboratory test, the "sender" looked at the image on the card, while the "receiver" tried to guess the image. They used twenty-five cards. The Rhines were among the first researchers to test ESP ability in a laboratory. And their results were significant. Some participant's scores were consistently high. The scores were higher than the odds one would get by guessing or by chance. Their research suggested that ESP ability is real. However, the Rhines were unable to get the same results in repeated studies and prove that ESP exists.

Since the 1930s, many scientists around the world have studied ESP. Several scientific studies show that some people seem to have psychic ability. However, there is no conclusive scientific evidence that fortune-telling is really possible.

Early Beliefs

Fortune-telling is not a new activity. Various forms of fortune-telling have been practiced for centuries in countries all over the world, including ancient Egypt, China, and Babylonia (current-day Iraq), going back to the year 4000 BC.

The earliest known form of fortune-telling was done in Mesopotamia, the site of many ancient civilizations, part of which is now known as Iraq. The people of Mesopotamia believed that gods and goddesses controlled all the events in the universe. They thought that weather events such as thunder and rain were caused by the gods and goddesses and foretold future events. The people of Mesopotamia believed that through the practice of **divination**, they could communicate with the spirit world. With divination, fortune-tellers use an object to help them focus their minds and make predictions about the future. People listened for predictions on the wind. They also observed the behavior of animals to tell the future.

A form of fortune-telling was also mentioned several times in the Old Testament of the Bible, in the "casting of lots." No one knows for certain what material was used for the lots, but Bible scholars think they were probably made of bone, wood, or jewels. The casting, or throwing, of lots was used in making decisions. The practice is similar to "drawing straws," flipping a coin, or rolling the dice in modern times. The casting of lots was also believed to be a form of divination. In the casting of lots and reading the result, people were letting a higher power make an important decision for them.

A modern version of the casting of lots is the Chinese I-Ching being practiced here to tell the future.

The casting of lots is also similar to the Chinese I-Ching, which is still practiced in modern times. With I-Ching fortune-telling, coins or special sticks are tossed. The pattern made by the items is read and interpreted to foretell the future.

Fortune-Tellers

A person with the ability to predict the future is known by various names. In modern times, a fortune-teller is sometimes referred to as a psychic. In ancient times, a fortune-teller was commonly called a prophet, seer, sage, or **oracle**.

An oracle is a person who predicts the future and gives advice. When fortune-telling, the oracle may go into a trance state to act as a medium who can receive information from the spirit world.

Oracles were consulted in many ancient civilizations, including Egypt, China, and Greece. Oracles are still used today. His Holiness the Dalai Lama, the spiritual and political leader of Tibet, consults two main oracles for guidance. One of the oracles is a young Tibetan woman called the Tenma Oracle. She

Animal Guts

The priests of Mesopotamia practiced hepatomancy. They studied the bumps and ridges in a sheep's liver to tell the future.

A statue in the temple of the state oracle of Tibet. This is the temple of the Dalai Lama's main oracle known as the Nechung Oracle.

lives with him in Dharamsala, India. The Dalai Lama's main oracle is a Tibetan monk known as the Nechung Oracle.

Tibetans consult oracles for a variety of reasons. They are not just used to foretell the future. They are also considered healers and protectors.

In his book, *Freedom in Exile: The Autobiography of the Dalai Lama*, the Dalai Lama describes what happens to the oracle when he is channeling the deity, or the godlike being from the spirit world. He wrote how the oracle, with his human body, can

A Presidential Prediction

Even President Abraham Lincoln believed in fortune-telling. A fortune-teller told Lincoln, at age 22, that he would one day be president of the United States.

barely contain the "volcanic energy" of the deity. The Nechung Oracle "moves and gestures as if his body were made of rubber and driven by a coiled spring of enormous power,"[1] said the Dalai Lama. Transmitting information from the spirit world can be very exhausting for the oracle. After giving a reading, the oracle needs to recover and rest.

In 2007 the Nechung Oracle visited eleven major cities in the United States. Inspired by information he received from the spirit world, the Nechung Oracle spoke about global warming and other important world issues. He asked people to take personal responsibility to protect the environment.

Chapter 2

Reading the Stars

A strology is a very old form of fortune-telling. Astrologists study the position of the planets with the belief that the planets' movements affect human behavior. Many people confuse astrology with **astronomy**, which is the scientific study of matter in outer space.

The practice of astrology began thousands of years ago. The oldest known records of astrology are from the second millennium BC in Mesopotamia. But scholars believe that astrology was practiced even before that time. A thousand years earlier, the ancient Sumerians, of the same geographic region, tracked the movement of the planets. The practice of astrology was later used in many ancient cultures, including Egypt, China, and India.

Astrologers in Babylonia developed the **zodiac**, which is related to astrology. The zodiac is an imaginary belt that stretches across the sky. The Sun and Moon and the major planets (such as Earth, Mercury, and Venus) move within this belt.

The early astrologers saw that the stars made images or shapes in the night sky. They called these shapes **constellations**. The zodiac belt is divided into twelve signs or houses, and each sign corresponds to a constellation. The twelve constellations within the zodiac were named, for example, "Scorpio" (shaped like a scorpion), "Capricorn" (goat), and "Pisces" (fish). A zodiac chart is a circular diagram that shows the twelve constellations.

By observing the constellations in the night sky, astrologers could track the movement of the planets and Sun through the zodiac and predict events on Earth.

Ancient beliefs in astrology led to the most popular form of astrology, which is still used today—the daily **horoscope**. Many people read their daily horoscope in the newspaper or on the Internet. A horoscope is a simple fortune based on a person's sun sign (where the sun was in the sky when the person was born). An astrological chart is more complicated. Besides the Sun, it involves the position of several planets at the time of someone's birth.

Looking to the Skies

Modern-day astrology is very similar to ancient astrology. An **astrologer** looks at a client's birth date. He or she then makes a chart that shows where the Sun, Moon, and eight major planets were located at the time of the person's birth. The position of the planets at the time of a person's birth is believed to influence a person's personality and life path. By looking at the current skies and the movements of the planets, an astrologer can forecast a person's future.

An Indian astrologer (left) reads a client's birth chart. The practice of astrology today is very similar to ancient astrology.

Because the creation of a birth chart is complex, some people use special computer software to create their chart. Others pay professional astrologers to create a thorough and precise astrological chart for them.

Johnny Depp's Birth Chart

Many astrologers have Web sites that advertise their services. AstroProfile.com is a Web site that offers celebrity astrology reports and a chart-making service to the general public. Like many astrologers and practitioners of fortune-telling, the astrologers on the Web site believe that a person's birth chart shows personality traits and patterns. They also believe that a person's future is not set in stone. For example, by changing a pattern, a person can change his or her life.

"We believe that observing your personal cycles can help you see your patterns and thereby make better decisions in your daily life,"[2] says the Web

It's All in a Name

The early astrologers named the planets after a god or goddess. They believed that each deity had a unique personality trait. They also believed that the gods and goddesses had power over events on Earth.

Johnny Depp's birth chart shows that he has a romantic nature and an appreciation for the arts. Birth charts can be used not only to tell the future, but also to show an individual's personality traits.

site astrologer who created a birth chart for *Pirates of the Caribbean* star Johnny Depp.

To create Depp's chart, the astrologer looked at Depp's exact birth time, date, and place. He saw that Depp was born in Owensboro, Kentucky, at 8:44 a.m., on June 9, 1963. The astrologer then calculated exactly where the Sun and Moon and eight major planets were in the sky at the time of Depp's birth.

This birth chart acted as a kind of map for the astrologer. It guided the astrologer and showed him what was happening in the skies at the exact moment Depp was born. The astrologer then interpreted the birth chart to discover things about Depp's personality and life path.

The position of the Sun and Moon are especially important in a person's birth chart. They hold the key to a client's personality. The other planets influence the Sun and Moon in subtle but powerful

Is Retrograde Unlucky?

Not all astrologers believe that Mercury in retrograde causes problems in communication and travel. These astrologers point out that retrograde movement of the planets is not unusual—the outer planets are in retrograde motion 40 percent of the time.

ways. "The planets are the antennae and arms of the horoscope, of which the body and soul are the Sun and Moon,"[3] said the astrologer.

Other factors influence an individual's horoscope. For example, the **ruling planet** of a person's birth chart is very important. Every person is thought to have a ruling planet that has special influence on his or her personality. Depp's ruling planet is Mercury. Mercury was the god of healing and business. The planet Mercury is associated with a keen business sense and the power to get things done in the world.

"[Depp hides] a world of determination under a very genial and apparently 'easy' exterior," said the astrologer. "No one can take advantage of him. Smart in business dealings, [he] comes across as friendly and carefree, but Depp is always paying attention. No one can take advantage of him, and he usually gets what he wants."[4]

Several parts of Johnny Depp's chart showed that he has a romantic nature and an appreciation for the arts. According to the astrologer, this position of the planets showed that Depp is "reserved but at the same time warm-hearted and affectionate."[5] It also showed that Depp has a deep appreciation for beauty, music, and the arts.

The chart, created after Johnny Depp became famous, revealed the personality traits that contributed to his acting success. His chart also showed that he is more than a celebrity—he is a kind and sensitive person, too.

The Power of the Planets

A professional astrologer named Donna was hired by a woman named Karin to create and read her birth chart in 2004. Karin was born on February 7, 1961, at 1:00 a.m. Karin's Sun sign was Aquarius,

Astrologers read astrological charts, such as the one pictured here, to find out general information about their clients' character and to foretell their futures.

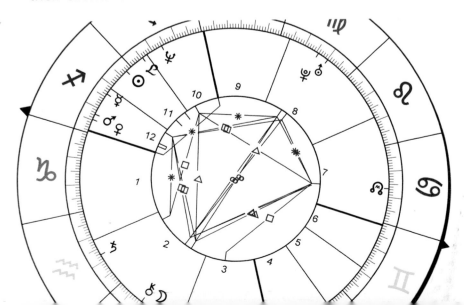

which told Donna lot about Karin's personality. People with the Sun sign Aquarius are known to be artistic and inventive, for example.

Donna discovered that Karin's Moon was in Libra. This told Donna that her client had a strong sense of right and wrong. She probably liked her home to be neat and tidy. Because of her gentle and friendly personality, she most likely had lots of friends.

Donna could tell general things about Karin's character through her astrological chart. She could also forecast future events in her life. By looking at current skies, and the position and movement of the planets, Donna could advise Karin about her future.

For example, Donna warned Karin that the planet Mercury was going into retrograde (a back-

Can Animals Tell the Future?

Some people observe the behavior of birds and other animals to tell the future. For example, some believe that seeing a white bird foretells a death. Other people believe that bird droppings landing on your head is good luck. Skeptics call these beliefs super-stitions.

ward movement) later in the month. Karin looked concerned. Donna told her not to worry, that this particular phase was temporary. She explained that the planet Mercury is associated with communication, travel, and business. When Mercury is in retrograde, people (not just Aquarians) can expect computers to break down, travel delays such as canceled flights and missed buses, and other hassles. Karin was glad for the warning and decided to put off her trip to visit her mother in Dallas until the following month. Her trip went smoothly, and she had a great time—with no bothersome problems like flight delays or lost luggage.

Predictions of Nostradamus

Some predictions made by astrologers have become famous. Michel de Notredame, commonly known as Nostradamus, was a well-known French astrologer of the 1500s. The predictions of Nostradamus are still widely respected, studied, and associated with world events today.

Some Nostradamus followers believe that he predicted the September 11, 2001, terrorist attacks on the United States. In particular, they say he foretold the devastating destruction of the World Trade Center towers in New York City. Nostradamus followers believed that the following translated excerpt from Nostradamus's writings predicted the attacks.

Earth-shaking fire from the center of the earth

Will cause the towers around the New City
  to shake:
Two great rocks for a long time will make
  war,
And then Arethusa will color a new river
  red.[6]

Some people believe that the writing seems to describe the events of September 2001. The "towers" refer to the twin towers of the World Trade

Some people believe that famous French astrologer Nostradamus actually predicted the 2001 terrorist attacks on the World Trade Center back in the 1500s.

Center, they believe. The "New City" refers to New York. Other scholars have found it significant that the letters of "the USA" are found within the word *Arethusa*.

Others, including both Nostradamus scholars and skeptics of the supernatural, believe that many writings of Nostradamus (including the example above) were not properly translated into English from the original French.

After the terrorist attacks of September 11, some Americans wondered if the attacks could have been foreseen or avoided by heeding the words of Nostradamus. Skeptics of Nostradamus's prophecies believe that some people have mistaken the meaning in his writings to try to make sense of a terrible tragedy.

Chapter 3

Messages in a Cup

Some fortune-tellers read tea leaves, coffee grounds, or even the leftover wine at the bottom of a wine glass. This method of fortune-telling is called **tasseography**. Tasseography has been practiced since ancient times in China, Greece, and the Middle East. Some people believe that travelers from the Middle East brought tasseography to Europe in the mid-1800s. The most common form of tasseography practiced in the United States is tea-leaf reading.

Tea-leaf reading is a method of divination. There are many little differences in tea-leaf readings. This is because every tasseographer has his or her own style of doing a reading. For example, one tea-leaf reader might have his client sip from her teacup before he reads her tea leaves. Another tea-leaf reader might ask the client to simply swirl the cup three times clockwise before he does a reading.

In every reading the tea-leaf reader is considered to be **intuitive**, or psychic. The reader focuses her mind as she looks for pictures in the scattered tea leaves. The images that she sees in the tea leaves tell her about the person's future. Readings have been done this way for hundreds of years all over the world.

A Personal Tea-Leaf Reading

In July 2007, 22-year-old Esther entered the door of a quiet Michigan café. She had come to get a tea-leaf reading from a tasseographer named Celeste.

Fortune-tellers may be able to predict an individual's future by reading the tea leaves left in a cup after the person has drunk the tea.

Esther's friends had told her about their experiences with the tea-leaf reader. They said that Celeste had given them information about themselves and their future that had really helped them.

Esther had never seen a psychic or a tea-leaf reader before. She had concerns about her future, so she thought she would give it a try.

Esther looked around the café. She found Celeste sitting at a back table reading a book. A cardboard sign was taped to her table that said, TEA LEAF READINGS $20.00, in fancy, purple handwriting.

When Esther approached Celeste's table, the tea-leaf reader looked up and smiled. Esther explained that she wanted a tea-leaf reading. Celeste invited her to sit down in the chair across from her.

Celeste poured her a cup of tea in a small, fragile-looking teacup that had pink roses on the outside. The cup was white on the inside. Esther could see a few loose tea leaves at the bottom of her cup. Celeste instructed Esther to drink about half a cup of tea while she pondered something that concerned her.

Esther took a few sips of tea while she thought about her relationship with her boyfriend, Jason. They had been dating for two years. He had said that he would like to marry her someday, but he was not ready. Esther was concerned that Jason had issues with commitment and that he might not ever be ready to marry her. "Will my boyfriend, Jason, and I get married?"[7] asked Esther.

What Do the Shapes Mean?

Below are a few examples of how a tea-leaf reader might interpret the shapes in the bottom of a teacup. These examples come from *Tea Cup Reading and the Art of Fortune-Telling by Tea Leaves*, which can be found on the Internet at www.gutenberg.org/ebooks/18241.

Basket = a new baby in the family

Car = wealth

Dragon = sudden changes

Flowers = a happy marriage

Lines = journeys and their direction

Moon = good fortune

Ring = marriage

Scissors = a quarrel or argument

Snake = illness

Star = good luck

Esther watched as Celeste picked up the teacup by the handle and swirled the contents of the cup three times counterclockwise. She then placed the teacup in the saucer. Celeste breathed deeply and glanced into the cup.

Celeste said that the first image she saw in the tea leaves was a ship. She explained that the ship could mean travel, or movement—perhaps even movement in a relationship. She also saw a star in the leaves, which she said was a sign of good fortune. Celeste remarked that the star shape had slowly changed into the number 2.

After a long pause, she said, "I see a woman dancing." She added that she felt intuitively that this was Esther dancing at her own wedding. "I am quite sure that you will marry your boyfriend—that is, if you feel the relationship is right for you! I see a happy couple."[8] Delighted with her reading and grinning from ear to ear, Esther thanked Celeste and gave her a crisp twenty-dollar bill.

As it turned out, life did not change for Esther right away. Almost two years after her tea-leaf reading, Esther and her boyfriend decided to get married. After the wedding they had a big reception—and did plenty of dancing.

Modern-day Witch Hunt

Not all fortunes lead to good outcomes, however. In 2007 the Israeli government charged a tea-leaf reader with practicing magic. Sana Kuma had practiced tasseography in Israel for nearly 25 years. Her clients included movie stars, models, and TV personalities. Reporter Dion Nissenbaum wrote in the *Seattle Times*, "Kuma was the target of a modern-day witch hunt."[9]

A woman receives a tea-leaf reading. Sometimes these readings do not have the positive results that the clients were expecting.

What They Want to Hear

Skeptics claim that fortune-tellers simply tell people what they want to hear. For instance, "You will come into a large sum of money," or, "You will soon meet the love of your life."

A man named Avraham Beihou brought the charges against Kuma. Shortly before his marriage, Beihou had hired Kuma to read his coffee grounds. Kuma told Beihou that she saw a "cursed bride" in the grounds. She advised him to get the curse removed, charging him $1,000 to bring in a man who specializes in removing curses. Beihou returned to Kuma for a second reading when his father was ill. Kuma went beyond the usual duties of a tasseographer. She sold him amulets (special objects believed to ward off evil) to protect his father for $2,200, but his father did not get well. Beihou felt angry and ripped off. He wanted justice. He hired a lawyer who filed charges against Kuma. The charges were later dropped when Kuma agreed to give back all the money Beihou had paid her.

"She has no talents—she can't heal people," said Beihou. "Every person can figure out a person, but only a doctor can heal someone. She can't."[10]

But still, Kuma has loyal customers who believe in her fortune-telling abilities. "She gives you ideas, names and events," said former Miss Israel, Nicole Halperin, "and when she gives you specific names and events, it makes you know that she's special."[11]

Chapter 4

In the Palm of Your Hand

Palm readers believe that information about a person and his or her future can be discovered on the hands. The lines, wrinkles, and **mounts**, or pads, in the palm of the hand may be clues to a person's past, present, and future. The shape of the palm and fingers may also tell a palm reader about a person's personality and character. Many people see palm reading as a form of amusement, but others take the ancient art very seriously.

Early Palm Reading

Palm reading, or palmistry, is also known as **chiromancy**. It began in India nearly 5,000 years ago. It was a part of a larger, mystical field of study called

32

Samudrik Shastra, which means "ocean of knowledge." Over time palm reading spread to ancient China, Egypt, and Greece. In Greece, palmistry was recognized by famous philosophers such as Plato and Aristotle.

Palmistry eventually traveled to Europe and the Western world. Palm reading was practiced during the Middle Ages in Europe. It received renewed popularity in Europe in the nineteenth century because of Count Louis Hamon (1866–1936). Hamon, known as "Cheiro," was one of the most charismatic and famous palm readers of the time. His popular book, *The Language of the Hand*, was published in England in 1896. Members of the British royalty and celebrities worldwide sought out Cheiro's palm-reading services.

Lend Me Your Hands

During a reading, the palmist usually looks at both hands. The dominant or **active hand** (the hand a person writes with) is thought to carry the most energy. The nondominant hand shows the genetic traits that people inherit from their parents.

This plastic hand shows the mounts of the palm used in palmistry, or palm reading.

The Cold Read

Skeptics say that some dishonest fortune-tellers use a technique called **cold reading** to fool their customers into believing they are psychic. Professor Morgan, the kindly fortune-teller in the movie *The Wizard of Oz*, did a cold reading on Dorothy. Marvel observed Dorothy's age, facial expression, and emotions. He then made a good guess that Dorothy had run away from home, and he convinced her that she needed to return home because Aunt Em was sick.

Palm readers who believe in **reincarnation** think that the nondominant hand shows traits from past lives, too. The active hand shows the palm reader what a person can create out of his or her life.

Similar to astrology, the mounts of the hand are named after planets that represent specific personality traits. A plump mount of Jupiter, for example, signifies a happy and honest person. The mount of Apollo shows an appreciation for beauty.

Lines That Tell All

The palm reader studies several lines in the hand but focuses on three main lines: the **heart line**, **head line**, and **life line**. The heart line is thought to represent love, romance, and the emotions. The line begins at the edge of the palm under the little finger and extends to the thumb. Palm readers often associate the head line with knowledge and communication.

The life line begins at the edge of the palm above the thumb and curves toward the wrist. The life line stands for a person's health and well-being as well as major life changes. Most palm readers agree that a broken life line docs not mean death. Instead the broken line shows a sudden and abrupt event in a person's life. A broken life line can mean the start or beginning of a relationship. It can also show an illness or a big move.

Actor Frank Morgan portrayed Professor Marvel in the 1930s film *The Wizard of Oz* and performed a cold reading on Dorothy to convince her to return home.

Many people think that a long life line means that a person will have a long life. But palm readers believe that a lengthy life line can be interpreted in various ways. For example, a long life line can indicate a long life, but it can also show a life full of adventure and good health.

Another important line is the **fate line**. The fate line can be traced from the bottom of the palm near the wrist. It runs up through the center of the palm toward the middle finger. This line shows important changes in life, both successes and challenges.

Carved in Stone?

Palm reader Thanu Pillay learned the ancient art from his uncle, Parameswaran Pillay, a well-known South Indian palmist. Pillay, who lives in California, takes his job seriously. He does not see palmistry as

Can Other Body Parts Be Read?

Palms are not the only part of the body that can be read by fortune-tellers. In China, face readers believe that much can be learned about a person's character by observing such things as the size of the earlobes or the shape of the nose.

entertainment or lighthearted fun. Instead he hopes to empower his clients with the self-knowledge they gain through a palm reading. "The information gained through a palm reading offers insight into the hidden potential of each person," says Pillay. "It also reveals our mental, physical, and spiritual strengths and weaknesses. We can use this knowledge to develop our personal goals that will ultimately shape our destiny."[12]

Like many palm readers, Pillay believes that the lines of the palm can change over time. "New lines may appear," said Pillay. "Old lines may fade or change."[13]

A Reading by Pillay

In July 1997 a middle-aged, married couple visited Pillay. The brown-haired, well-dressed man did not say a word. His wife, a confident blond-haired woman, did all the talking. She asked Pillay to give her husband a palm reading. She especially wanted information about his future in business.

Pillay agreed and carefully examined the palms of the silent, well-groomed stranger. The first thing he noticed were the full, rounded mounts and strong, deep lines in the man's palms. "Mounts are reservoirs of energy," said Pillay. "Deep lines are powerful."[14]

Pillay noted that the man's thumb had a firm joint (not very flexible or bendable). This showed that the man had strength of character and stubborn determination. His thumb was long, which told Pillay that the man was outgoing, independent, and dynamic. The man's Jupiter and Sun mounts were very full. This told him that the man had great ambition and desire for power.

He looked closely at the man's dominant hand. His fate line was deep and straight. His Saturn mount was very full. Both signs showed Pillay that the man would have career success.

"You will be holding very high positions in your career," Pillay told him, gazing at the man's palms. "You will achieve your ambitions through your extraordinary leadership qualities."[15]

People, such as the man pictured here, have several reasons for having their palms read, which may include learning about the future or just having fun.

When the reading was done, the man's wife thanked Pillay. The mysterious man smiled but never said a word. Several months later, Pillay saw the man on television. He was being interviewed by a TV journalist. He was the president of a major international oil company.

In His Own Hands

Gerard, a palm reader in Honolulu, Hawaii, works out of a small office in the front of his house. In the spring of 2008, a young man named Joshua arrived at Gerard's office. Gesturing to a small table by a front window, Gerard asked Joshua to sit down and make himself comfortable. He looked carefully and thoroughly at both of Joshua's hands before speaking.

Gerard noted that Joshua had a long, deep, and clearly marked life line. This showed strong health and lots of energy. He also noted that Joshua's life line lifted up past his thumb, which meant that he had a positive attitude about things. He saw good fortune in Joshua's work life.

Gerard noticed that Joshua's head line was long and straight. This showed clear and logical thinking. Gerard pointed out that Joshua knew what he wanted in life and knew how to get it.

Joshua wanted to know about his love life. In particular, he wanted to know if his love interest, who had broken up with him a few months earlier, would come back to him. Gerard looked carefully at Joshua's heart line. He noted that it started between his middle and

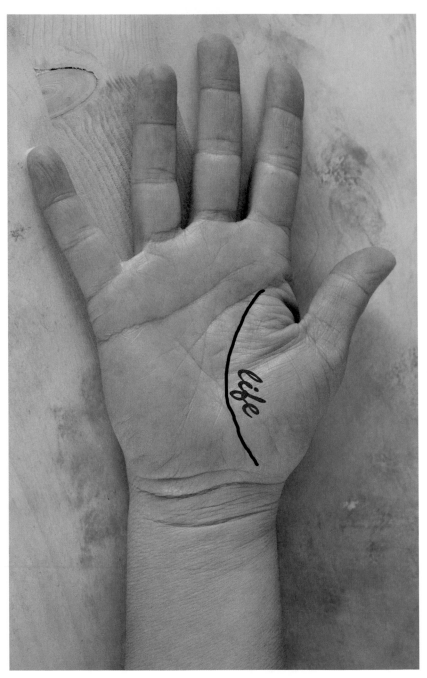

The life line used in palmistry is highlighted on this palm. The life line stands for health, well-being, and major life changes.

index finger. This, he figured, meant that Joshua gave his heart away too easily. He also noted that Joshua's heart line was chained (it had many small lines criss-crossing the line), which indicated nervous emotions and romantic drama.

Instead of making a prediction about Joshua's love life, Gerard simply reported what he saw in Joshua's palms. Like many fortune-tellers, Gerard believes that the choices people make in their present lives shapes their future. He assured Joshua that the power to change his life was literally in his own hands.

For the rest of the day, Joshua pondered the results of his palm reading. Gerard was right, he thought. The relationship had been full of drama. He had not been happy. Joshua thought about what he really wanted and deserved. A few months later, Joshua met a person who was easy to be with and made him laugh. They are still together.

People hire fortune-tellers for various reasons. Some people want to know about future events. Others see fortune-tellers because they want to reflect on their lives. They want to think about where they are at the moment and where they are going. Even if a person does not believe in the ability to foresee future events, it can be fun to see a fortune-teller.

Notes

Chapter 1: Predicting the Future

1. "Nechung—The State Oracle of Tibet," The Government of Tibet in Exhile, the Official Agency of His Holiness the Dalai Lama in London. www.tibet .com/buddhism/nechung _hh.html.

Chapter 2: Reading the Stars

2. Quoted in "Heaven Over All: Astrology Report for Johnny Depp." AstroProfile.com. June 19, 2004. www.astroprofile.com/celastropdf/DeppOverAll .pdf.
3. Quoted in "Heaven Over All."
4. Quoted in "Heaven Over All."
5. Quoted in "Heaven Over All."
6. Morgana's Observatory, "Century 1, Quatrain 87." Nostradamus 1997–2006. http://paranorm al.about .com/gi/dynamic/offsite.htm?zi=1/XJ/Ya&sdn= paranormal&cdn=newsissues&tm=46&gps=39_ 350_1140_724&f=10&su=p284.8.150.ip_&tt=14 &bt=0&bts=1&zu=http%3A//www.dreamscape .com/morgana/titan.htm.

Chapter 3: Messages in a Cup

7. Celeste. Telephone interview with author, February 15, 2008.
8. Celeste, February 15, 2008.
9. Quoted in Dion Nissenbaum, "Israel Prosecutes That Old Black Magic," *Seattle Times*, July 22, 2007. http://seattletimes.nwsource.com/html/nation world/2003800298_fortune22.html.
10. Quoted in Dion Nissenbaum, "Israel Prosecutes That Old Black Magic," *Seattle Times*, July 22, 2007.

http://seattletimes.nwsource.com/html/nation
world/2003800298_fortune22.html.

11. Quoted in Dion Nissenbaum, "A Modern Day
Witch Hunt," Checkpoint Jerusalem Blog. July 17,
2007.

Chapter 4: In the Palm of Your Hand

12. Thanu Pillay, e-mail interview with the author, July
11, 13, and 14, 2008.
13. Thanu Pillay.
14. Thanu Pillay.
15. Thanu Pillay.

Glossary

active hand: The dominant hand read by a palm reader.

astrologer: A person who practices astrology.

astrology: The study of planets in the belief that their movements affect human behavior.

astronomy: The study of the structure and movement of the celestial bodies.

character reading: Fortune-telling that is done to reveal information about a person's character or personality.

chiromancy: The art of telling the future through the study of the palm.

cold reading: A technique that fortune-tellers use to discover details about people in order to convince them that they know more about them than they really do.

constellations: Images or shapes that astrologers see in groupings of stars.

divination: When fortune-tellers use an object to focus their mental or psychic energy.

extrasensory perception (ESP): Communicating or knowing something by means other than the five physical senses.

fate line: The line of the palm that shows important changes in life.

head line: The line in the palm associated with knowledge and communication.

heart line: The line in the palm that represents the heart and emotions.

hepatomancy: Studying the liver of sheep to tell the future.

horoscope: A prediction of future events based upon a person's birth sign, their astrological chart, and the position of the planets.

intuitive: Psychic; having the power to receive information through a "gut feeling."

life line: The line of the palm that represents health and well-being and major life changes.

mounts: Pads in the palm of the hand that are read by palm readers.

oracle: A person who communicates with the spirit world in order to predict the future or give advice.

parapsychology: A branch of psychology that deals with the study of psychic phenomena (such as ESP) that have not been explained by scientists.

psychics: Fortune-tellers in modern times.

reincarnation: Rebirth in a new body or another form of life.

ruling planet: A planet that is thought to have influence over a particular sign of the zodiac.

superstitions: Beliefs or notions not based on reason or knowledge.

tasseography: The reading of tea leaves, coffee grounds, or sediment at the bottom of a glass.

zodiac: An imaginary belt stretching across the sky that contains the twelve astrological constellations, or a circular diagram representing the twelve astrological signs.

For Further Exploration

Books

Madalyn Aslan. *What's Your Sign? A Cosmic Guide for Young Astrologers.* New York: Grosset & Dunlap, 2002. This colorful book introduces astrology to young readers and includes a zodiac spin wheel so they can find fun facts about their astrological sign.

Karen Gravelle. *Five Ways to Know About You.* New York: Walker & Company, 2002. This informative book introduces readers to astrology, palm reading, numerology, Chinese horoscopes, and handwriting analysis.

Vernon Mahabal. *The Secret Code on Your Hands: An Illustrated Guide to Palmistry.* San Rafael, CA: Mandala Publishing, 2002. This colorful book was written by an experienced palm reader.

Terry O'Neill. *Fortune-Telling (Fact or Fiction?),* Farmington Hills, MI: Greenhaven Press, 2006. Readers can further explore the mysteries of fortune-telling in this book.

Web Sites

Palmistry International (http://palmistryinternational .com). This Web site includes articles about palmistry and offers a free palm reading techniques section.

The Skeptiseum: The Skeptical Museum of the Paranormal (www.skeptiseum.org). This online museum offers a skeptic's view of many fortune-telling methods.

Index

Picture Credits

About the Author

Katherine E. Krohn is the author of many books for young people. Krohn is also a tea-leaf reader, an I-Ching practitioner, and a tarot-card reader. She has a dog named Lucky, a black cat named Ursula, and a Maine Coon cat named Moon Pie. She lives with her family in Oregon. Readers can find out more about her and her books at www.katherinekrohn.com.